ESPECIALLY
for
MISSIONARIES

ESPECIALLY *for* MISSIONARIES

Volume 1

Using the Book of Mormon as a Key to Conversion

Ed J. Pinegar

Covenant Communications, Inc.

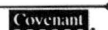

Grateful appreciation is expressed to Grant V. Harrison, who provided material for me when this was given as a talk.

Published by Covenant Communications, Inc.
American Fork, Utah

Copyright © 1997 by Ed J. Pinegar
All rights reserved

Printed in the United States of America
First Printing: September 1997

04 03 02 01 00 99 98 97   10 9 8 7 6 5 4 3 2 1

ISBN 1-57734-139-2

USING THE BOOK OF MORMON AS A KEY TO CONVERSION

A Divine Witness

The Book of Mormon was translated by the power of God through the Prophet Joseph Smith, who gave his life for this book. He was tarred and feathered and left for dead in Hyrum, Ohio; he was thrown in jail and mocked and ridiculed just for bringing the book into existence. And Joseph wasn't the only prophet who suffered for the sake of the book. Abinadi was burned at the stake. Enos prayed to the Lord with all of his heart that the book would come forth in this day. "Thy fathers have also required of me this thing," the Lord told Enos. "And it shall be done unto them according to their faith; for their faith was like unto thine" (Enos 1:18).

The prophets in Book of Mormon times wrote in the language of reformed Egyptian characters, but this is a book for our dispensation. Joseph Smith called the Book of Mormon the keystone to our religion, and then declared that "a man would get nearer to God by abiding by its precepts, than by any other book" (Book of Mormon, Introduction).

If you know anything about building arches, you know that the keystone is the piece of stone that holds the arch up. The purpose of the Book of Mormon is to witness that Heavenly Father is our Father and that he is good to us and loves us; to witness of Jesus Christ; and to document how he has dealt with all of his people. This book is for you and me; it is written for members and nonmembers alike. If you learn to love it, this book will be the greatest power you have on your mission. If you learn to love the Book of Mormon and understand its teachings, you will then be able to testify of the book, and you will have great converting power. You will never be the missionary you were destined to be until you love and live this book. It is the key to your converting power. It is the key to your retaining power. It is the key of our dispensation.

The purpose of the Book of Mormon is fivefold. First, it stands as a second testament or witness for Jesus Christ. Second, it authenticates the Bible. Third, it shows the goodness of God to his children. Fourth, it makes people aware of the promises that God has made to his children. And fifth, it restores to earth many plain and precious truths that have been lost since the fulness of the gospel existed.

The first purpose, however, is primary. This book convinces people, both members and nonmembers, that Jesus is the Christ. "Come unto Christ, and be perfected in him" (Moroni 10:32) the scriptures invite. That is the purpose of the Book of Mormon. That is what you must know, that is what you must feel, that is what you must understand. That knowledge of the book must be radiating from your very being. This is one of the reasons that you are instructed to sup from these pages for thirty minutes every day.

Loving and Sharing the Book

The Book of Mormon will never live in your life until you delight in the word of God. "Now, we will compare the word [the Book of Mormon is the word of God] unto a seed," Alma teaches in Alma 32:28. "Now, if you give place, that a seed may be planted in your heart. . . ." In other words, we take this seed, this word of God, this Book of Mormon, and put it in our hearts. (It might help to know that in Hebrew the word *heart* is *leb* or *lebab*, which interpreted means the center of the mind or the center of the soul, the decision-making center of your body.)

When we yield our hearts to the Lord, what are we doing? In essence we're saying, "All my decisions are the decisions you would make, Father. Not my will, but thy will."

Now back to Alma. If we give a place for the seed, which is the Book of Mormon, to be planted in our hearts (or in other words, all of our decisions will be made by the principles contained in the book), then "if it be a true seed, or a good seed, if ye do not cast it out by your unbelief, that ye will resist the Spirit of the Lord, behold, it will begin to swell within your breasts; and when you feel these swelling motions, ye will begin to say within yourselves—It must needs be that this is a good seed, or that the word is good, for it beginneth to enlighten my understanding, yea, it beginneth to be delicious to me" (Alma 32:28).

When the Book of Mormon lives in our lives, then we will be pure disciples of Christ with great converting power, fulfilling the destiny that President Ezra Taft Benson described so eloquently when he said, "I have a vision of homes alerted, classes alive, pulpits aflame, with the spirit of the Book of Mormon message. I have a vision of the whole church getting nearer to God by abiding the precepts of the Book of Mormon." (General Conference, October 1988)

President Benson has also said, "The Book of Mormon needs to become more central in our preaching, our teaching, and our missionary work" (*Ensign*, May 1986, pp. 5-6). He counseled us to flood the earth with the Book of Mormon, adding this call to action: "I challenge our mission leaders to show their missionaries how to challenge their contacts to read the Book of Mormon and pray about it. I challenge the homes of Israel to display on some of their walls, great quotations and scenes from the Book of Mormon." (General Conference, October 1988)

In early Church history, some missionaries returned from their missions and were reproved. "You have treated lightly the things you have received," they were told. "Which vanity and unbelief have brought the whole church under condemnation" (D&C 84:54-55). President Benson echoed this reproof when he told Church members that "the Book of Mormon has not yet, nor is yet the center of our personal study, and our preaching and our missionary work, and of that we must repent" (General Conference, April 1986)

"The Book of Mormon contains that portion of the Lord's word which is needed to prove the divinity of this great latter-day work, and which is needed to teach the basic doctrines of salvation to mankind" said Elder Bruce R. McConkie. (*Ensign*, June 1980, p. 56) And President Marion G. Romney said, during General Conference in 1960, that "The Book of Mormon is the most effective piece of missionary literature we have." President Ezra Taft Benson promised that "The Lord will manifest the truthfulness of it, by the power of the Holy Ghost." (General Conference, April 1986)

A Powerful Tool of Conversion

It's important that you and I develop an abiding faith in the Lord's promise that if people will ask with a sincere heart, having faith in Christ, the truthfulness of the Book of Mormon will be given to them. (See Moroni 10:3-5.) Think about what it means to our investigators if they can accept the Book of

Mormon in their lives: If the Book of Mormon is true, then Joseph Smith was a prophet. If Joseph Smith was a prophet, the First Vision really did take place. If the First Vision was reality, the priesthood was restored. If the priesthood was restored, the Doctrine and Covenants, Pearl of Great Price, and other scriptures are true. Not only that, but the Church, which was established by Joseph Smith, is true. And that's not all! We're led by true prophets of the Lord today. They will know all that when they accept the Book of Mormon.

This is what we must engrain in our very souls: The Book of Mormon is the tool that will retain converts better than any other thing. If we root the people to our sociality, or friendliness, or love, we root them to us instead of to Christ. That happens sometimes because missionaries are so loving and so good.

But that's exactly why we must put the Book of Mormon first. If we root them to that holy book of scripture, our converts will be retained long after we leave. I'm sure you've heard of converts who have left the Church as soon as "their" missionaries have been transferred. That doesn't happen when converts have come unto Christ, because coming unto Christ goes much deeper than simple friendship. You see, loving Christ is the essence of conversion. We are converted to Jesus Christ by the power of the Holy Ghost, which is felt as we study and pray about the Book of Mormon, because the Book of Mormon is a sure witness and testament that Jesus is the Christ. Any other root will wither.

When we root our converts in the love of the people or the love of the Church or the love of the sociality and friendships they feel at church, what happens the first time they feel a lack of love? They fall away. Can you remember a time in your life when you didn't feel loved? You felt lonely, sorry for yourself, maybe even physically sick. But when we are rooted in Christ and his love, we are rooted in something solid and secure, because Christ's love never changes; it's always there. The love of our Heavenly Father is the same.

The Book of Mormon plays a crucial role in rooting people to Christ. Every aspect of a person's testimony is anchored in place by the Book of Mormon. Think of that: every aspect of a person's testimony is held in place by what is found in the pages of the Book of Mormon.

The degree to which we effectively help people understand how the Book of Mormon fulfills the Lord's divine purposes is the same degree to which we will see them become convinced that Joseph Smith was a prophet. That's the same degree to which they will be committed to continually praying and studying the Book of Mormon. And soon they will see that the Book of Mormon does lead them to Christ. So you can see the purpose and power of the Book of Mormon, the keystone of our religion.

Delighting in the Word of God

Remember that before our investigators can sense the power and divinity of the Book of Mormon for themselves, they must sense it in us. We must delight in the word of God. We must love the Book of Mormon. We must feast upon its words.

When the Book of Mormon becomes delicious to you, you will sparkle. You will be excited. You'll visit your investigators and say, "Oh, I just had to drop by and read you this part here; this is so good I can hardly wait to tell you!" If you don't feel that way, your investigators won't feel that way. Now perhaps you can begin to understand why one precious half-hour every day is spent supping from the pages of this book of books. Learn to love the book, and you'll not only love to live its teachings yourself, but you'll love to teach it.

President Benson said, "I would particularly urge you to read again and again, the Book of Mormon and ponder and apply its teachings." (General Conference, April 1986) Isn't that interesting? Ponder and apply its teachings. I try to do that every day, pondering the scriptures every night and then applying a scripture in my life every day, and even recording it in my journal. This daily application of scriptures can absolutely change our lives.

I taught the Book of Mormon at BYU for sixteen years, and I was always astounded when I would talk about something in class and a student would observe, "Oh, I read that once."

"Oh, you read it once?" I would reply. "Well, I teach this book every year and find things I've never even seen before. And you've read it once?"

So, we had an assignment. I gave extra credit to students who read 2 Nephi 9 or Enos for thirty days in a row before going to bed. A student once asked me: "Why? Why do we need to read it every day? I mean, I'll get it after just a night or two."

"You just read it and see," is all I answered.

Well, one day I was walking to class, and all of a sudden this young man was waiting for me by the door. He literally leapt upon me, gave me a hug and said, "Oh, Brother Ed, Brother Ed, it's true, it's true!"

I said, "I know it's true, Elder."

"I understand what you mean now," he said. "I read Enos, and on the twenty-first day something happened inside. I wanted everybody to be converted. Brother Ed, I'm thinking of checking out of school and going on my mission today."

"Can't you just wait two more weeks until the semester ends?" I asked.

This young man fell in love with the Book of Mormon because he did what the prophet said, again and again and again, and then he applied it in his life. Until we apply it to our lives, we will not delight in it. We will not enjoy this feeling. We will not be enthusiastic about it. We'll say, "Yeah, I read the book this morning." But when we love it, we'll live it because we apply it.

Nephi understood this principle: "For my soul delighteth in the scriptures, and my heart pondereth them" (2 Nephi 2:15). President Benson also understood: "Reread the Book of Mormon so that we might more fully come unto Christ, be committed to him, centered in him, and consumed in him." (General Conference, October 1987)

Do you see now what will happen with your investigators? When Christ comes into our lives, we are born of God, and we'll also be strengthened through the Book of Mormon. If we are conscientious in our study of the Book of Mormon, we will not be susceptible to Satan's enticings. I promise you that if you'll earnestly and prayerfully ponder and steadfastly read the Book of Mormon and live it, the adversary will have no effect upon you. And unless you do that, you will not be strong.

Why is this? How do we become spiritually strong? How do we grow in faith? The answer is always the same: The word of God applied in our lives makes us strong. It makes our spirits strong; our spirits grow in strength when we sup from the pages of the Book of Mormon. There is power in the book that begins to flow into our lives the moment we begin to seriously study the Book of Mormon. We will find greater power to resist temptation. We will find the power to avoid deception. We will find the power to stay on the straight and narrow path. These are promises President Benson has given us.

If we truly delight in the word, we are worthy to be instruments in the Lord's hands. And then we will know that the power of the word is the greatest power to change people's lives. (See Alma 31:5.)

Now I'm going to make a profound statement, based upon my experiences as a missionary and a mission president: We convert people like us. What we are is what our converts want to be. So, if our light is a dim light, they will be a dim convert. If our light is strong, they will see Christ in us.

The Savior said, "Behold, I am the light which ye shall hold up, that which ye have seen me do, behold, ye see that I have prayed unto my father and ye all have witnessed" (3 Nephi 18:24). In other words, the light that we have, the light that we possess, the light that we hold up, is our conversion to Christ. So it's natural that our converts like what we like, that they want to do what we do. If we are rooted in the Book of Mormon, that's what they will want to have. If we are not rooted to the Book of Mormon, chances are they will be rooted to something else, and when the whistling winds of the world come by, all of a sudden they will wither and even die. It's that precious; it's that critical.

When we truly delight in the word, our ability to motivate our investigators to read the Book of Mormon will be enhanced significantly. In other words, when we delight, they'll be delighted. Every day, we should have a goal to place so many copies of the Book of Mormon. You'll begin to see the importance of the book and the role it plays in callbacks and other teaching appointments.

Faith and Persistence

Now, we have the book and its power. We are beginning to see what we need to do to be the kind of missionaries that Christ would have us be. We need to be full of excitement, full of enthusiasm, full of love for the Book of Mormon.

Once we're well on the road to developing those characteristics, how are we going to find people to teach? Whenever we are deceived, whenever we are discouraged, we will lose our motivation; and when our motivation decreases, our work ethic also decreases or disappears.

When I worked on the Church Missionary Training Committee, I would train mission presidents during the mission presidents' seminar. In preparation for that training, I surveyed mission presidents already out on assignment and asked them what their main responsibility was. "Motivating missionaries is ninety-five percent of my work," they almost always replied. "Missionaries get discouraged, they get tired, they get worn out."

Guess why? Where were they rooted? Not in the Book of Mormon. Do you see how you can prepare now? You'll become so strong and so magnificent that the Lord will take you and use you because you're rooted to Christ. When another door slams, you'll say, "Great, let the door slam. Hit me. That will really give me a blessing, you know. Throw water on me, anything. I need the blessings." And if you have that kind of positive attitude, you'll be marvelous.

We should approach our work with the faith that if we persist in our efforts to find people to teach, the Lord will prepare a way for people to accept us. If we believe that, it will happen. If we doubt it, I promise you it will not happen, and we will have a difficult time finding investigators. But if we believe it can happen, if we believe with faith that we can baptize and that the book will bring people unto Christ, it will happen.

I testify to you that if you are exactly obedient, continuously, steadfastly, you will reap the harvest the Lord intended you to have. Plead with the Lord every day. Cultivate the power of discernment to know the will of the Lord, and to be led to those who are the elect of God.

Use the Book of Mormon effectively in your efforts to get people to listen to your message. Ask them, "If you knew there was another book written that talked about Jesus Christ and what he did, would you like to read that? You would? Well, I just happen to have five copies of that very book right here in my pocket."

It is so easy. Plead with the Lord to soften the hearts of the people and open their hearts, that they will receive you. Exercise your faith. The Lord promised that he would go before you to prepare the hearts and the minds of the people to accept the gospel. He said he would guide you to those he's prepared or will lead them to you. (D&C 84:85-88, 1 Nephi 4:6)

Here is one of the most beautiful parts of the process. If you've studied, if you've pleaded with the Lord, and if you're worthy and desire righteousness, things will come out of your mouth that you've never even known.

The other day I was speaking to a group, and afterwards a man came up to me and said, "That was the most profound statement I've ever heard in my life."

"What was?" I asked.

"When you said, 'Truth without testimony is hollow.'" He had it written down on a piece of paper.

"Wow," I said. "Who said that?"

"You did."

"When?" I asked.

"Just now, in that room."

"Can I write that down?" So I wrote it down, and now I'm sharing it with you. And why was I able to say that? Because the Lord inspires us; sometimes we don't even realize what we said! President Marion G. Romney once observed that he always knew when he had spoken by the Spirit because he learned from what he had said.

When we exercise our faith, the Lord will bless us. If our faith is sufficient, those beyond the veil, under the direction of Jesus Christ, will assist us in our missionary labors (see D&C 49:27 and Moroni 7:30-31). I believe that; I know it's true.

Helping Investigators to Know

When you place a copy of the Book of Mormon, the investigator needs to feel your love so that you can both feel the Spirit. And after you've placed the book, always quietly pray in your heart and mind, "Is there something from the Book of Mormon that I could share with them that would touch their heart to bring them closer to God?" This needs to be in our minds every moment of every day. We never take that out of our minds. We never replace it with anything. *Is* there something from the Book of Mormon I could share with them that would cause them to want to change?

Of course, we first get a promise from them to read the book, and then we must schedule a follow-up visit. If we fail to get a follow-up visit, and then if we fail to follow up on the reading assignment, our investigator begins to think, "Don't tell me how much you want me to read this book. You asked me to read 1 Nephi 3:7, but you didn't even ask me the next time when you came whether I'd read it or not. And I stayed up late after bowling to read it! But you don't even care whether I read it or not."

When you mark those scriptures for your investigators to read, write it in your planner: "Friday 7 p.m, Anderson Family. 1 Nephi 3:7 and all of 2 Nephi 9." You can even write notes about why you made particular assignments: "They were interested in the Atonement of Christ, so we invited them to read 2 Nephi 9 and Alma 40. They also were very interested in faith, so we assigned Moroni 7. And of course we had them read Moroni 10:3-5."

Now we've placed the book and we're faithfully following up on reading assignments. Next, we must teach investigators what they must do in order to qualify themselves to know that it's true.

Many missionaries tell their investigators to "Pray about the Book of Mormon and you can know if it's true or not." But they leave out a crucial step. Our investigators must qualify themselves to receive an answer from the Lord. They must study and pray, and then the Lord will tell them it's true. We must learn that principle: Our investigators need to qualify themselves to receive their answer from the Lord.

This is how we help them qualify themselves. First, we ourselves must establish a pattern of reading the Book of Mormon regularly. We must have a special feeling about the book. We must have a clear understanding about Moroni 10:3-5 and explain that passage to our investigators in detail when we introduce the book.

We need to explain to them that when they're reading is when the Lord will testify to them it's true. They don't read all 531 pages and then say, "Okay, I've finished reading. Now I pray." It's an ongoing daily process to know that the Book of Mormon is true. Make sure investigators understand that they don't need to wait until they've finished reading to start asking! To help them understand that, read through Moroni 10:3-5 with them, discussing specifically the following things: How the hand of God brought the book forward originally; how it was prepared by the prophets; how it came forth through Joseph Smith; and how it might be possible that the Lord has prepared them to find the Book of Mormon.

When investigators begin to read the book, they rehearse what they've learned—how merciful the Lord is, how he's been involved in the affairs of the people, what the prophets have done. As they read, investigators will remember these things; they are then prepared to feel good as they read. Then we can explain to them that all good comes from a loving Heavenly Father and his beloved Son, Jesus Christ.

If our investigators are sincere after we've carefully followed these steps, things will begin to happen. They will ponder and pray about the contents of the Book of Mormon, and its teachings will become important in their lives. When Parley P. Pratt received the Book of Mormon, he said that he couldn't eat or sleep; all he wanted to do was read the book. Parley P. Pratt was sincere and qualified to receive an answer from the Lord. If our investigators are sincere, they'll ponder the contents of the Book of Mormon, and by means of the Spirit, they will agree with the teachings.

In Galatians 5:22, we read: "But the fruit of the Spirit is love, joy, peace, longsuffering, gentleness, goodness, faith."

When our investigators feel these things as they read the Book of Mormon, they'll feel the Spirit and know that the book is true. Sometimes our investigators are unfamiliar with the Spirit, and they need a little help identifying where these wonderful feelings come from.

"How do you feel when you read the Book of Mormon?" you might ask them.

"Good," they'll answer.

"All good comes from our Heavenly Father," you'll teach. "And those feelings are a witness that the Book of Mormon is true." The greatest tool we have to bring people unto Christ is the Book of Mormon.

Here are some things that our investigators will feel as they read: They'll understand the glorious truths; they'll recognize particular doctrines; they'll know that it's uplifting and inspired. We must not fail to teach our investigators to recognize the witness of the Spirit.

The teachings of the Book of Mormon are logical and rational. They correspond with the Bible in many ways, and we can use that as we teach investigators who are familiar with the Bible.

Have you ever taught or been with someone when they have taught about a gospel principle, and the investigator says, "Well, that's what I've always believed"? But when you ask them what church they belong to, you discover that particular church doesn't even teach the principle in question.

Why is that? Because we all came to this earth with knowledge gained from the pre-earthly existence. And when we hear it repeated here, our heart resonates to it. The elect of God hear these teachings, and they find the teachings appealing. They experience a spiritual uplift.

One of the greatest truths we'll ever teach people is that they are children of God the Father and that he has a plan that provides us eternal life and happiness. This is fundamental to the gospel of Jesus Christ and is taught in the first discussions. So many people in the world don't even realize this. And when we teach this to people and they pray about it, the Lord will tell them it's true; they'll receive answers and know that the doctrine is right.

Investigators tend to seek a sign when they are praying about the Book of Mormon. They want lights to go on three times in succession or a visitation from an angel or something like that. We must not look for incredible signs when we're seeking to discover truth, but we must recognize the signs from the Spirit. That's why we, along with our investigators, must understand Galatians 5:22 and recognize these signs.

The Spirit is the key. We must preach with love and concern, tenderly, and as Alma counseled his sons, with soberness—then it will be easier to have the Spirit. Do not contend, and do not Bible-bash. Simply teach the Book of Mormon. There are more than two hundred different sects in the world today that believe the Bible. Preach from the book that was brought forth for our dispensation, and let the Spirit bear witness of that book. Then the Spirit can also bear witness to the truthfulness of the Bible, as far as it is translated correctly. But the truthfulness of the Book of Mormon is the key, and we must help our investigators gain that knowledge.

The Power of Working Together

Don't overlook the power of working with members. If you want extra power, delegation is a great tool for getting things accomplished. God the Father delegated the creation of the earth to his son, Jehovah, who with Michael and others organized this earth from material that had always existed. Then, under the direction of the Father, our first parents were created.

I believe in delegation; I believe that many hands make light work. If I were on a mission, I would work with members in the ward or branch I was serving in. I'd find five or ten people, and I'd develop relationships of trust with them. I'd visit them, get to know them, prove my righteousness and let them see my sincere desire.

Then I'd approach them. Every member is a result of missionary work, and most members have had a missionary experience. Share with these people or these families your own missionary experiences. Ask them to share their conversion story with you. Tell them about one of the people you've just recently converted. Tell them about the greatest work in the world. Tell them what a joy it is to work with people who are eager to hear about the gospel. Tell them how wonderful it is to be associated with people who are searching for the truth.

As we share these missionary experiences, the Spirit of the Lord will come upon us. Read Alma 6:6 and 3 Nephi

18:19-23 with these members, then invite them to help you with your work. Ask them to help you find people to teach, help you friendship and fellowship the people you are teaching now.

During a mission presidents' seminar in June of 1980, President Kimball promised Church members that if they would pray night and morning regarding their desire to see other people join the Church, the Lord would hear their prayers and soften the hearts of the people they associate with. Invite your member friends to pray every day for this blessing, and promise them that when they pray with all their hearts, with real intent, they'll see a difference as the hearts of their friends and associates are touched and softened.

I bear witness that the gospel of Jesus Christ is true. The Book of Mormon is the Lord's book—the book for our time to bless his children. We must learn to use it on a daily basis with everyone we teach, utilizing the commitment pattern. If you do that, I know the Lord will bless you.

Other titles by Ed J. Pinegar

Tapes

Being a Missionary
Especially for Missionaries, vols. 1-6
Happily Ever After
Hope in Christ
Man Is that He Might Have Joy
More Especially for Missionaries, vols. 1-2
Overcoming Twelve Tough Temptations
Personal Success, Win! Win!
Pleasing God
Power Tools for Missionaries (1-4)
Succeeding at Life, One Step at a Time
Turn it Over to the Lord

Booklets

Especially for Missionaries Booklets (1-4)

About the Author

Ed J. Pinegar served as president of the Missionary Training Center in Provo from 1988-1990. He was the president of the London South Mission from 1985-1988. His wife, Pat, is the Primary general president. Ed and Pat, parents of eight children, reside in Provo, Utah, where Ed teaches at the UVSC Institute of Religion.